POSH POOCHES

ACKNOWLEDGMENTS

The author would like to thank Joelle Hoverson, Linda Niemeyer, Beth Casey, Rachel Casparian, KJ Swanson, Anne Hill, Niegel Smith, Martha Bernabe, and Brian McNorrill—and, of course, trixie + peanut!—for their help with this book.

This edition published by Barnes & Noble, Inc., by arrangement with Nancy Hall, Inc.

2005 Barnes & Noble Books

Copyright © 2005 Nancy Hall, Inc.
All rights reserved.
10 9 8 7 6 5 4 3 2 1
ISBN: 0-7607-7313-0

Designed by Atif Toor and Mark Weinberg
Technical editing by Edie Eckman
All dog photos © trixie + peanut, inc.

Printed in China

POSH POOCHES

12 knitting patterns for the well-dressed dog

Written by Kimberly Hamlin
Dog Photography by Louis Irizarry
Knitting Photography by Susan McCartney

BARNES & NOBLE
NEW YORK

PAGE 19

PAGE 35

PAGE 47

PAGE 71

PAGE 79

CONTENTS

INTRODUCTION	6
ABBREVIATIONS/SYMBOLS	12
OBLIQUE RIB SCARF SET	15
BASIC SWEATER	19
BASEBALL JERSEY	25
EMBROIDERED DOG BED	31
SUPER-WARM BULKY SWEATER	35
POLO SHIRT	41
RIBBON DRESS	47
BULL'S EYE	53
HERRINGBONE JACKET	59
ARGYLE SWEATER	65
HOODIE	71
PATCHWORK BLANKET	79
KNITTING TECHNIQUES	86
INDEX	94
ABOUT THE AUTHOR	96
ABOUT TRIXIE + PEANUT	96

PAGE 65

INTRODUCTION

SIZING AND MEASURING

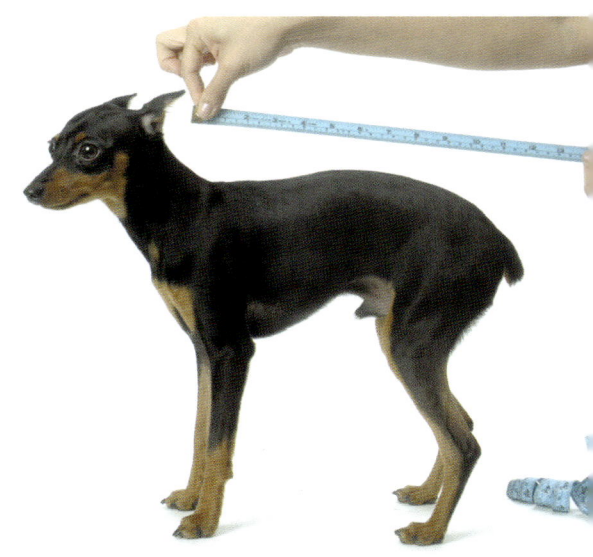

The patterns in this book are constructed around a basic set of sizes, 8–28, which directly correspond to back length. In other words, a size 8 measures 8 inches from neck to tail, a size 10 measures 10 inches from the base of the neck to the tail, and so on. Measure your dog's back length in inches and this will be the size to follow throughout the book.

Many patterns are written in a range of sizes. Numbers for the smallest sizes will be given first, with the others following in order within parentheses. Before you start knitting, you may want to circle the numbers for your own size throughout the pattern.

Sizes: 8 (10, 12, 14, 16, 18, 20, 22, 24, 26, 28)
The sizes will always be written in this order throughout each pattern. If your size is not listed, it means a pattern was not written for that size.

Chest and belly measurements vary from pattern to pattern, so it is always best to check the finished diagrams to see what size will work best for your dog. If your dog is between sizes, it is generally better to go with the bigger size.

NEEDLES

There are almost as many kinds of knitting needles as there are knitters. Of course, the needle choice is up to you. If you are new to knitting, be aware that it takes a while to get used to knitting needles in general, so try not to get overwhelmed. Take time to test out new needles. You never know what needles might best suit you until you try them.

Needles come in three basic formats: straight, circular, and double-pointed. Straight needles are the most common. These needles are perfect for knitting flat pieces and come in a variety of lengths and materials such as bamboo, aluminum, wood, plastic, and sometimes glass. Collectable vintage needles can be found in steel, bone, or even ivory. Circular needles are two needle points connected by a flexible cable. Nowadays, they are most commonly made of aluminum or bamboo, but older versions might be made of plastic. Circular needles are used for knitting in the round, which could be used for some of the sweaters in this book. Many knitters prefer circular needles for their convenience during travel.

Double-pointed needles come in sets of four or five needles, with points on both ends. You'll find them in all the materials listed for straight needles and in a variety of lengths. While you could knit an entire dog sweater on double-pointed needles, it's best to use them for smaller circles—like necks, sleeves or cuffs. Socks, mittens, and gloves are other items that are often knitted on double-pointed needles.

The needles included in this kit are size US #9 (5.5mm). These needles will work for most knitters for these seven patterns: Oblique Rib Scarf Set, Basic Sweater, Baseball Jersey, Embroidered Dog Bed, Herringbone Jacket, Hoodie, and Patchwork Blanket.

STANDARD YARN WEIGHT SYSTEM

Yarn Weight Symbol	1 SUPER FINE	2 FINE	3 LIGHT	4 MEDIUM	5 BULKY	6 SUPER BULKY
Types of Yarn in Category	Sock, Fingering, Baby	Sport, Baby	DK, Light Worsted	Worsted, Afghan, Aran	Chunky, Craft, Rug	Bulky, Roving
Suggested Knit Gauge Range in Stockinette Stitch to 4 inches	27–32 sts	23–26 sts	21–24 sts	16–20 sts	12–15 sts	6–11 sts
Recommended Needle in US Size Range	1 to 3	3 to 5	5 to 7	7 to 9	9 to 11	11 and larger
Recommended Needle in Metric Size Range	2.25–3.25 mm	3.25–3.75 mm	3.75–4.5 mm	4.5–5.5 mm	5.5–8 mm	8 mm and larger
Posh Pooch Projects using these weights	Herringbone Jacket	Ribbon Dress	Bull's Eye	Argyle Sweater, Baseball Jersey, Basic Sweater, Hoodie, Oblique Scarf	Embroidered Dog Bed, Patchwork Blanket, Polo Shirt	Super-Warm Bulky Sweater

GAUGE

So, you've just bought the greatest yarn and can't wait to begin knitting when *boom!* you remember that thing called gauge. Do not skip checking your gauge!

You may be thinking, "But I bought what the pattern said . . . same yarn, same needle size . . . I'm ready to begin!" Nope. You're not. There's a little bit of work you must do before you cast on for real.

Gauge is the number of stitches that equals 1 inch of knitting. Often gauge is written as the number of stitches that equals 4 inches.

Like handwriting, everyone's knitting is a little different. Many people say, "I usually knit pretty much on gauge." This might be true for a couple of items you made, but with all the patterns out there, written by numerous designers, you can't expect to match gauge every time. You have to take time to check your gauge for every project. To do this, you must make a gauge swatch.

MAKING A GAUGE SWATCH

Start with the suggested needle size and cast on several stitches. A good starting point is about 20 stitches, but the more generously sized the gauge swatch, the better. It is best to have a swatch big enough to measure in more than one place. This results in a more accurate gauge measurement.

Usually gauge is given in stockinette stitch (knit one row, purl one row) but sometimes, if a different stitch is used in the project, the gauge will be given in that pattern stitch. Work the swatch in the pattern stitch called for in the gauge statement. Don't assume that stockinette stitch gives the same gauge as your pattern stitch.

After you've knit about 4 inches, stop to measure the swatch. With a ruler, measure 4 inches and count how many stitches are in those 4 inches. If the number matches your pattern instructions, you're ready to begin. If you have too many stitches, change to a bigger needle size and try again. If you don't have enough stitches, try again with smaller needles. Knit at least 4 inches more and check the gauge again. Keep trying until you get the correct gauge.

Take a look at these two squares. Both squares measure 4 inches but the first is only 8 stitches while the second is 16 stitches. It is important that you match the gauge of your pattern to ensure a properly fitting garment.

POOCH PROFILE: LUCY

Feisty one-year-old Jack Russell Terrier Lucy has many reasons to smile. When just weeks old, Lucy experienced a reaction to her puppy shots and nearly died. After spending over a week in the hospital, she completely recovered and is now a happy, healthy, and lovable pet to her devoted parents. Known for her sunny disposition, Lucy loves to chase balls anywhere, any time! She indulges in scrambled eggs and the occasional filet mignon. Like her mother, she enjoys shopping and is a frequent visitor to the trendiest boutiques in Manhattan where she always receives the four-paw treatment.

ADJUSTING A PATTERN TO FIT YOUR DOG

We've done our best to create a group of patterns to fit a variety of dogs, but if you're having trouble finding a good fit, here are a few ideas for adapting sizing.

Length is generally easy to adjust. Simply take out or add an inch or two in an area without shaping. Double-check the diagrams provided to locate these sections. If you keep other elements such as shaping and leg openings the same, and remember to modify the same amount in all pieces, you'll have success.

Changing width is a little more difficult because you can't just change the number of stitches without some preplanning. Our suggestion is to find the written pattern that best fits the width of your dog. You can then adjust the length to fit him or her properly. Depending on their level of experience, most knitters are more comfortable controlling length rather than width. If you do venture into adjusting the width, make sure to read through the entire pattern first and make a note of where you'll need to make changes. Take notes to limit frustration along the way.

WASHING

Clothes made for your pet will probably need to be washed often. When picking yarns for these projects we've kept laundry needs in mind. Many cottons and superwash wools will withstand regular machine washing, using a gentle cycle and cool water and machine drying on low heat. Other yarns require a bit more attention, but are not the headache some like to imagine. For these yarns, use cool water, but don't let it run directly over your knitting.

There are several types of detergents made specifically for gentle cycles or wool so the choice is up to you. Lavender Woolwash, which simply requires soaking but not rinsing, is a favorite.

To hand wash, fill a tub or sink with water and the recommended amount of detergent. Place the item in the water and swish it around gently. After it soaks for a while, lift it out carefully, supporting its weight. Squeeze out the excess water and roll the item in a clean, dry towel. Pin it into shape, if necessary, on another dry towel and let it dry flat. This method is safe for all knitted items.

ABBREVIATIONS / SYMBOLS

CC	Contrasting color
dec	Decrease
k	Knit
k1f&b	Knit into front and back of stitch (an increase)
k2tog	Knit next 2 stitches together (a right-leaning decrease)
k2togtbl	Knit next 2 stitches together through back loops (a left-leaning decrease)
m	Meters
MC	Main color
m1	Make one by picking up the bar running between stitches and knitting into the back of it
p	Purl
p1f&b	Purl into front and back of stitch (an increase)
p2tog	Purl 2 together (a decrease)
pm	Place marker
rep	Repeat
RS	Right side
sl1	Slip 1
ssk	Slip, slip, knit (a left-leaning decrease), slip next 2 stitches one at a time as if to knit, insert left needle back into these stitches and knit them together
sts	Stitches
tbl	Through back loop
WS	Wrong side
yb	Yarn back between the needles
yds	Yards
yf	Yarn forward between the needles
yb	Yarn back
yo	Yarn over
Block	Shape finished pieces to their proper measurements. See finishing/care for more information.

SKILL LEVELS

 Easy—Suitable for beginners. Only knit and purl with little or no shaping required.

  Intermediate—Requires skills beyond the basics, such as knitting in the round, using multiple colors, and picking up stitches.

   Advanced—Meant for experienced knitters. May include slightly difficult stitch patterns, color patterns, shaping, and tricky sewing.

Chew on This!

The term oblique means that the axis is not perpendicular to the base. So, the ribbing actually goes diagonally across the piece. Oblique can also refer to the set of muscles that form the lateral walls of our abdomens – as well as the type of sit-ups that target those particular muscles!

OBLIQUE RIB SCARF SET

Knitting a scarf is quite possibly the easiest place to begin. This particular pattern has a unique diagonal ribbing that can be elegant or manly. As an added bonus, the doggy version has a convenient slit to keep the scarf from coming untied while your pooch darts about. Using a hand-dyed yarn such as the Lobster Pot yarns lends excitement and a depth of color to your project.

OBLIQUE RIB SCARF SET
[FITS MOST DOGS AND ADULTS!]

Sizes:
Adult—One size fits all
Dogs—Small/Medium (Medium/Large)

Yarn: Lobster Pot Yarns Worsted (85% wool, 15% mohair, 188 yds/ 172 m), 2 skeins for adult and small dog scarf, 2 skeins for adult scarf, 1 skein for dog scarf.

Lobster Pot Yarns are produced by a small operation and vary in weight and yardage.

Yarn Weight:

Gauge: 16 sts = 4″ (10 cm) in Oblique Rib Pattern

Needles: One pair straight needles size US #9 (5.5 mm) or size needed to obtain correct gauge

Other: Tapestry needle

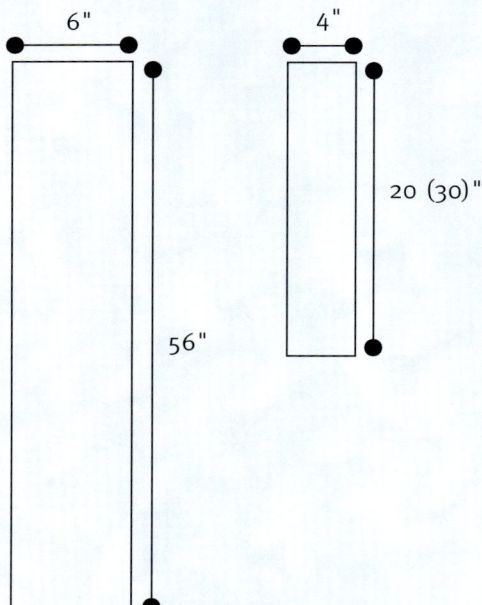

DOG SCARF

Cast on 16 sts. Work in Oblique Rib Pattern for 5 (7)", ending with a right side row. Continue in pattern across 4 sts, bind off 8 sts, work pattern across remaining 4 sts. Next row: Work pattern across 4 sts, cast on 8 sts, work pattern across remaining 4 sts. Continue in pattern until piece measures 20 (30)".
Bind off in pattern. Weave in tails.

OBLIQUE RIB PATTERN (multiple of 4)

Row 1 (RS): *K2, p2; rep from *.
Row 2: K1, *p2, k2; rep from * to last 3 sts, p2, k1.
Row 3: *P2, k2; rep from *.
Row 4: P1, *k2, p2; rep from * to last 3 sts, k2, p1.
Rep Rows 1-4.

ADULT SCARF

Cast on 24 sts. Work in Oblique Rib Pattern until piece measures 56" from beginning.
Bind off.
Weave in tails.

Top dogs **Peanut** *and* **Lucy** *know it's all about the accessories!*

Chew on This!

Using different colors for the body and chest panels can really liven up this piece. One way to decide which two colors you want to pair is to use a color wheel. Color wheels show the relations among colors. Any two colors that lie opposite from one another are called "complementary colors." Complementary colors usually go well together!

BASIC SWEATER

This sweater is designed in two pieces, the main body and a smaller chest panel, using Manos del Uruguay yarn. Creating the chest panel separately allows you to adjust the chest width and leg openings to custom-fit your dog. If your dog is wider than the pattern allows, simply follow directions for the correct size chest panel, adjusting length as necessary. This effortless pattern has plenty of room for personal touches. We suggest having fun with color to really make it your own!

BASIC SWEATER

[GREAT FOR ALL DOGS]

Sizes: 8 (10, 12, 14, 16, 18, 20, 22, 24, 26, 28)

To fit chest: 8-9 (10-11, 12-13, 14-15, 16-17, 18-19, 20-21, 22-23, 24-25, 26-27, 28-29)"

Yarn: Manos del Uruguay (100% handcrafted, kettle-dyed, pure wool, 3.5 oz/100 g; 138 yds/126 m), 1 (1, 1, 2, 2, 2, 3, 3, 4, 4, 4) skeins.

Try using multicolor yarn or buying several colors for unique stripes.

Yarn Weight:

Gauge: 16 sts and 22 rows = 4" (10cm) in stockinette stitch

Needles: One pair straight needles size US #9 (5.5 mm) or size needed to obtain correct gauge [OPTIONAL: Sizes 20–28 may use a 24" (60 cm) size US #9 (5.5 mm) circular needle to accommodate the large number of stitches.]

Other: Tapestry needle, split ring markers, stitch holder

Note: Slip stitches as if to purl throughout pattern.

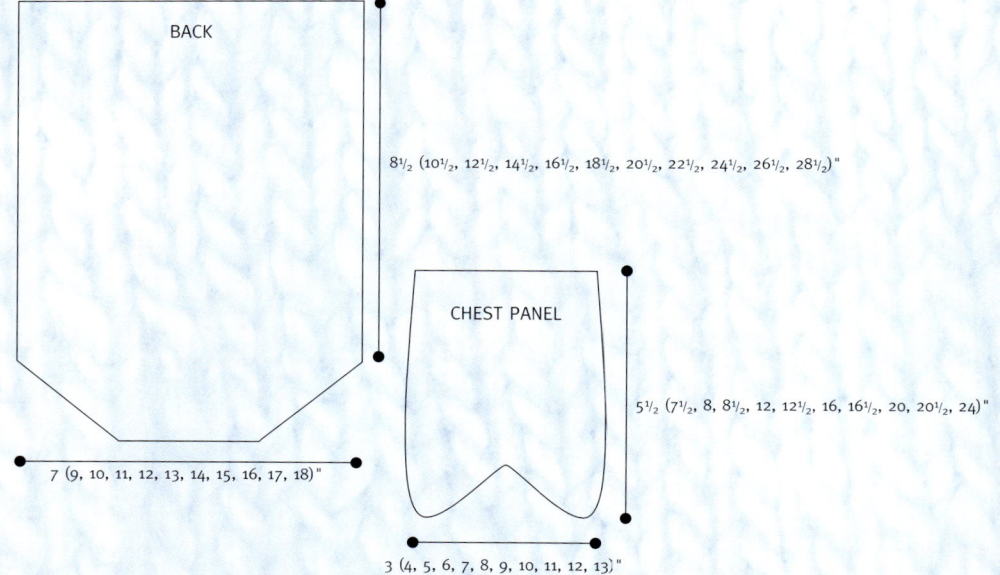

BODY

Cast on 20 (28, 28, 28, 36, 36, 44, 44, 52, 52, 60) sts.

Row 1 (RS) * K1, p1; rep from *.

Rows 2-5: Rep Row 1.

Increase for Belly

Row 1: Sl1, knit to end.

Row 2: Sl1, purl to end.

Row 3: Sl1, k1, m1, knit to last 2 sts, m1, k2. [22 (30, 30, 30, 38, 38, 46, 46, 54, 54, 62) sts]

Row 4: Sl1, purl to end.

Rep these four rows 3 (3, 5, 7, 5, 7, 5, 7, 5, 7, 5) more times. [28 (36, 40, 44, 48, 52, 56, 60, 64, 68, 72) sts]

At this point, place a split ring marker on left and right edges of work to mark the start of middle section. This is necessary in order to determine the proper length of chest panel later.

Rep Rows 1 and 2 until work measures 7 1/2 (9 1/2, 11 1/2, 13 1/2, 15 1/2, 17 1/2, 19 1/2, 21 1/2, 23 1/2, 25 1/2, 27 1/2)" from beginning, ending with a purl row.

Optional Leash Opening

Sl1, k12 (16, 18, 20, 21, 23, 25, 27, 28, 30, 32), bind off 2 (2, 2, 2, 4, 4, 4, 4, 6, 6, 6) sts, k13 (17, 19, 21, 22, 24, 26, 28, 29, 31, 33).

Sl1, p12 (16, 18, 20, 21, 23, 25, 27, 28, 30, 32), p12(16, 18, 20, 19, 23, 25, 27, 29, 30, 30, 32), cast on 2 (2, 2, 2, 4, 4, 4, 4, 6, 6, 6) sts, p13 (17, 19, 21, 20, 24, 26, 28, 29, 31, 33), p13 (17, 19, 21, 20, 24, 26, 28, 30, 31, 31, 33).

Work even until piece measures 8 1/2 (10 1/2, 12 1/2, 14 1/2, 16 1/2, 18 1/2, 20 1/2, 22 1/2, 24 1/2, 26 1/2, 28 1/2)" from beginning.

Place stitches on a stitch holder. These stitches will become the neck.

There's nothing "basic" about **Wyatt** *in this adorable sweater!*

CHEST PANEL

Cast on 13 (17, 21, 25, 29, 33, 37, 41, 45, 49, 53) sts.

Next row: Sl1, purl to end.

Next Row: Sl1, k1, k2tog, k2 (4, 6, 8, 10, 12, 14, 16, 18, 20, 22), m1, k1, m1, k2 (4, 6, 8, 10, 12, 14, 16, 18, 20, 22), ssk, k2.

Rep these two rows until piece matches back from split ring marker to neck stitches on holder.

Next row:

Sizes 8-20: K1, *p1, k1; rep from *.

Size 22: K1, *(p1, k1) 3 times, p1, k2tog; rep from * to last 4 sts, (p1, k1) 2 times.

Size 24: K1, *(p1, k1) 3 times, p1, k2tog; rep from * to last 8 sts, (p1, k1) 4 times.

Size 26: K1, *(p1, k1) 2 times, p1, k2tog; rep from * to last 6 sts, (p1, k1) 2 times.

Size 28: K1, *(p1, k1) 2 times, p1, k2tog; rep from * to last 3 sts, p1, k1, p1.

[13 (17, 21, 25, 29, 33, 37, 37, 41, 43, 46) sts]

Join Chest to Main Body

Place stitches from stitch holder back on needle. Continue across these stitches as follows:

Sizes 8–22: Continue in established 1 x 1 rib to last 2 sts, p2tog.

Sizes 24: *(P1, k1) 3 times, p1, k2tog; rep from * to last stitch, p1.

Size 26: *(P1, k1) 2 times, p1, k2tog; rep from * to last 5 sts, (p1, k1) 2 times, p1.

Size 28: K1, *(P1, k1) 2 times, p1, k2tog; rep from * to last stitch, p1

[40 (52, 60, 68, 76, 84, 92, 96, 98, 102, 108) sts]

Cookie (far left) snuggles up with her posh pals in one of our cozy, easy-to-knit, basic sweaters.

Neck

Continue in established 1 x 1 rib until neck ribbing measures 3 (4, 4 1/2, 5, 5, 5, 6, 6, 6, 7, 7)" or desired length. Bind off loosely in rib.

Finishing

Block pieces. Sew neck seam using mattress stitch. Try the sweater on your dog to determine proper location for leg openings.

It might be a little difficult to get your dog to stay still enough to measure, but it only takes a second to mark the chest panel. Enlist some help to get him to roll over and show his belly!

Leaving a 1/2" allowance above and below the dog's leg, use split ring markers to mark the top and bottom of leg opening.

We recommend being generous with the leg openings. (We all know what it's like to have a tight shirt restrict your arm movement!) You want your dog to be comfortable, so leave plenty of room. You can always make it smaller later.

Do not sew the area between markers. Simply seam on either side of the leg opening using mattress stitch. (See page 86 for instruction.) Weave in ends. Make another one!

Chew on This!

A jersey is a basic, knitted fabric that does not have ribs (or "ridges"). Original jerseys were made out of wool and were worn by English fishermen. Jerseys can be smooth or they can have a sort of hairy texture.

BASEBALL JERSEY

Remember those old faded pictures of your uncle's softball team? Ever wish someone had been sentimental enough to save those awesome jerseys along with all the trophies and dirty softballs? While nothing can quite compare to those old tees, Blue Sky Alpacas' newest collection of cottons are great. This pattern is perfect for beginning knitters, because the raglan sleeve is easy to master, the yarn quick to knit with, and the gauge is so common that you'll be able to remake warmer versions in all kinds of other yarns.

BASEBALL JERSEY

[SMALL TO LARGE DOGS]

Sizes: 8 (12, 16, 20, 24)

To fit chest: 8-10 (10-14, 14-18, 18-22, 22-26)"

Yarn: Blue Sky Alpacas Blue Sky Cotton (100% cotton, 3.8 oz/ 110 g, 150 yds/138 m), 1 (1, 1, 1, 2) skein Color A, 1 skein Color B

Yarn Weight:

Gauge: 16 sts and 22 rows = 4" (10 cm)

Needles: One pair straight needles size US #9 (5.5 mm) or size needed to obtain correct gauge

Other: Tapestry needle, crochet hook size H (4.5 mm) for neck

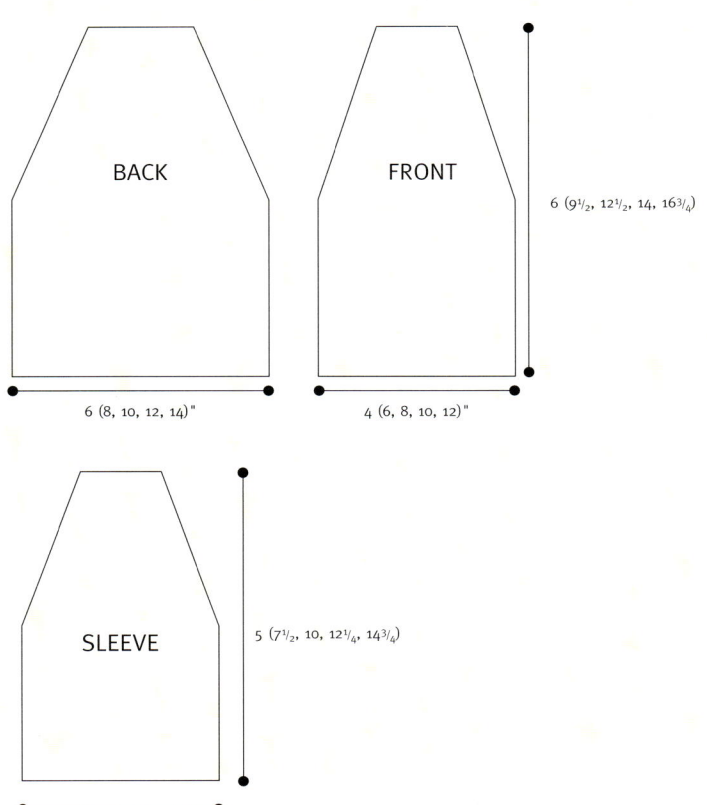

BACK

With A, cast on 18 (24, 32, 38, 46) sts.

Row 1: (RS): Knit to last stitch, m1, k1.
Row 2: Purl to last stitch, m1, p1.
Rep these two rows 2 (3, 3, 4, 4) more times. [24 (32, 40, 48, 56) sts]
Work even in stockinette stitch until piece measures 3 (4 1/2, 6 1/2, 7, 8)" from beginning, ending with a wrong side row.

Raglan Decrease

Row 1: K2, ssk, knit to last 4 sts, k2tog, k2. [22 (30, 38, 46, 54) sts]
Row 2: Purl.
Row 3: Knit.
Row 4: Purl.
Rep last four rows 3 (5, 7, 9, 11) more times. [16 (20, 24, 28, 32) sts].
Bind off.

Chico steps up to the plate. Your dog can step up to the plate, too.

FRONT

With A, cast on 10 (16, 24, 30, 38) sts.

Row 1: (RS): Knit to last stitch, m1, k1.

Row 2: Purl to last stitch, m1, p1.

Rep last two rows 2 (3, 3, 4, 4) more times. [16 (24, 32, 40, 48) sts]

Work even in stockinette stitch until piece measures 3 (4 1/2, 6 1/2, 7, 8)" from beginning, ending with a wrong side row.

Raglan Decrease

Row 1: K2, ssk, knit to last 4 sts, k2tog, k2. [14 (22, 30, 38, 46) sts]

Row 2: Purl.

Row 3: Knit.

Row 4: Purl.

Rep last four rows 3 (5, 7, 9, 11) more times. [8 (12, 16, 20, 24) sts]

Bind off.

SLEEVE (make two)

With B, cast on 16 (20, 28, 32, 40) sts.

Work even in stockinette stitch until piece measures 3 (3, 4, 5, 6)" from beginning, ending with a wrong side row.

Raglan Decrease

Row 1: K2, ssk, knit to last 4 sts, k2tog, k2. [14 (18, 26, 30, 38) sts]

Row 2: Purl.

Row 3: Knit.

Row 4: Purl.

Rep last four rows 3 (5, 7, 9, 11) more times. [8 (10, 12, 12, 16) sts]

Bind off.

Finishing

Block all pieces.

Using mattress stitch, sew raglan seams. Sew side seams along straight edges, from end of Front/Back increasing to armhole. Sew sleeve seams.

Right side facing, with B, work one row of single crochet around neck in sleeve color.

Weave in ends.

POOCH PROFILE: WYATT

Tiny terrier Wyatt is a one-year-old Yorkie who weighs in at a whopping three pounds. A true ladies' man, Wyatt's penchant for making out in public has gained him many admirers and sealed his reputation as a charming Casanova, not to mention as one of the best kissers in New York City. Fearless, fashionable, and proudly metrosexual, Wyatt lives a luxurious lifestyle that includes an extensive trixie + peanut wardrobe, a strict beauty regimen, and a gourmet raw diet, all thanks to his devoted mom. When not breaking hearts at the dog run, Wyatt spends his time jet-setting from coast to coast.

Chew on This!

Dogs aren't the only ones who like to sleep in style! Ancient Egyptians once slept on low couches with fancy legs that were shaped like animals. In the 15th century, people began enclosing their beds in drapes. The hangings kept sleepers warm, in addition to giving the beds below a ceremonial importance.

EMBROIDERED DOG BED

If you're having trouble finding a dog bed that suits your sense of style, it's time to make one yourself! Lorna's Laces produces awesome hand-dyed yarns that can be tossed right into the washer and dryer. With the number of stunning colors available in this yarn, you're sure to find a match for both your pet's personality and your décor.

EMBROIDERED DOG BED

[GREAT FOR ALL DOGS]

Sizes: Extra Small (Small, Medium, Large)

Finished Measurement: 18 x 18 (22 x 22, 26 x 26, 32 x 32)"

Yarn: Lorna's Laces Shepherd Bulky (100% Superwash wool, 4 oz/ 113 g, 140 yds/128 m), 4 (6, 8, 12) skeins, 1 skein CC.

Because this is a hand-dyed yarn, dye lots may vary significantly. Most yarn stores are willing to special order enough yarn for you. However, if you're unable to acquire enough of the same lot, work two rows in one skein and two rows in another to blend them together. Another hint: Buy extra yarn. You can always use it for another project!

Yarn Weight:

Gauge: 16 sts and 22 rows = 4" (10 cm) in stockinette stitch

Needles:
For sizes Extra Small, Small and Medium, one 24" (60 cm) circular needle size US #9 (5.5 mm).
For Large, one 32" (80 cm) circular needle size US #9 (5.5 mm)

Other: One 16 (20, 24, 30)" square pillow form, tapestry needle, pins

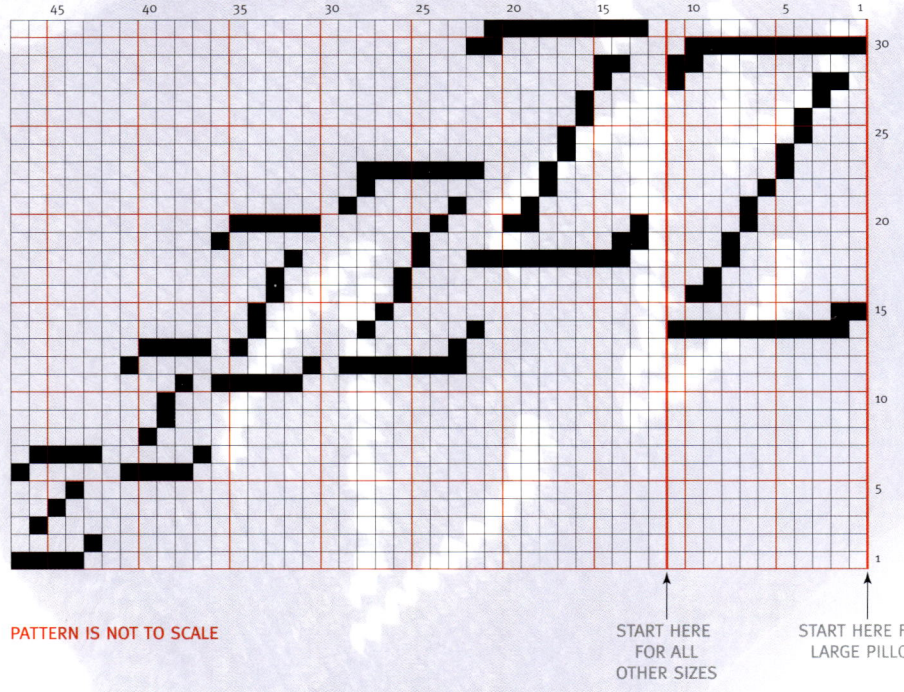

PATTERN IS NOT TO SCALE

START HERE FOR ALL OTHER SIZES

START HERE FOR LARGE PILLOW

FRONT

Cast on 72 (88, 104, 128) sts.

Knit 8 rows (4 ridges) for border.

Row 1: Knit.

Row 2: K4, purl to last 4 sts, k4.

Rep Rows 1 & 2 until piece measures 17 (21, 25, 31)" from beginning.

Knit 8 rows (4 ridges) for border. Bind off.

BACK (make two)

Cast on 52 (60, 68, 80) sts.

Knit 8 rows for border.

Row 1: Knit.

Row 2: K4, purl to last 4 sts, k4.

Rep Rows 1 & 2 until piece measures 17 (21, 25, 31)" from beginning.

Knit 8 rows for border.

Bind off.

Finishing

Following chart, starting in the upper right corner with largest Z, embroider pattern to pillow top using duplicate stitch. Secure all ends.

With wrong sides together, pin front and back pieces together, overlapping back panels to match right and left edges of front. Use backstitch to sew along the inside of garter stitch edging (see dotted line). This will leave a 1" border around pillow.

16 (20, 24, 30)"

18 (22, 26, 32)"

Make sure your seam is secure where the back panels overlap, as this will get the most wear inserting and removing pillow form.

If your stitches are quite uneven you may block the pieces. However, you may find that stretching the fabric to fit the pillow form will be enough to neaten things up.

Sweet dreams for **Peanut**.

Chew on This!

Siberian or Alaskan huskies do well in extremely cold weather. In fact, they are often the breeds of dog selected for Iditarod racing. The Iditarod is the world's most famous sled dog race. The course covers about 1,100 icy miles and crosses two Alaskan mountain ranges. The Iditarod starts on the first Saturday of March every year in Anchorage.

SUPER-WARM BULKY SWEATER

This easy-to-make sweater is similar to the basic pattern, but in a much bigger gauge. Because it's worked in one piece, you'll love how quickly this knits up. Alpaca is one of the warmest natural fibers, so it's perfect for freezing winter nights or playing in the snow. Pick up extra yarn to make a matching hat and scarf for yourself so you won't get jealous of your warm doggy.

SUPER-WARM BULKY SWEATER
[GREAT FOR BIG BIG DOGS & LITTLE LITTLE DOGS]

Sizes: 8 (10, 12, 24, 26, 28)

Yarn: Blue Sky Alpacas Bulky (50% alpaca, 50% wool, 3.5 oz/ 100 g, 45 yds/41 m), 1 (1, 2, 5, 6, 6) skeins

Yarn Weight:

Gauge: 8 sts and 10 rows = 4″ (10 cm) in stockinette stitch

Needles: One set US #15 (10 mm) double-pointed needles, one 24″ (60 mm) circular needle size US #15 (10 mm). [OPTIONAL FOR SIZES 24–28: One 16″ (40 mm) circular needle for neck stitches] Sizes 8–12 can be completed entirely on double-pointed needles.

Other: Stitch markers, tapestry needle

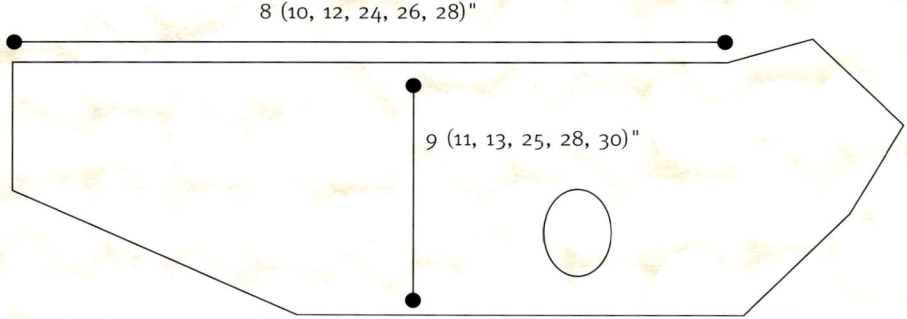

SWEATER

With circular needle, cast on 10 (14, 14, 30, 32, 34) sts. Do not join.

Purl 1 row.

Next row: K1, m1, purl to last stitch, m1, k1. [12 (16, 16, 32, 34, 36) sts]

Next row: P2, knit to last 2 sts, p2.

Rep last two rows 3 (3, 5, 9, 11, 12) more times, ending with an increase row. [18 (22, 26, 50, 56, 60) sts]

Sizes 8–12 only: Distribute stitches evenly on three double pointed needles.

All sizes: Join into round.

Purl all rounds for 3 (3, 4, 8, 9, 9)″ more.

Leg Openings

Next round: P2 (2, 2, 5, 5, 5), bind off 3 (3, 3, 5, 5, 5) sts, purl to last 5 (5, 5, 10, 10, 10) sts, bind off 3 (3, 3, 5, 5, 5) sts, purl to end of round.

Next Row: P2 (2, 2, 5, 5, 5), turn.

Next Row: K4 (4, 4, 10, 10, 10), turn.

Sizes 24–28 only: *P10, turn. K10, turn; rep from * once more.

All Sizes:

P4 (4, 4, 10, 10, 10), cast on 3 (3, 3, 5, 5, 5) sts over opening, purl to next opening, cast on 3 (3, 3, 5, 5, 5) sts, purl to end of round.

Continue purling until piece measures 8 (10, 12, 23, 25, 27)″ from beginning.

POOCH PROFILE: MAC

Handsome Mac is an extraordinarily talented three-year-old Jack Russell Terrier. Splitting his time between his homes in New York City and Greenwood Lake, Mac is a true Renaissance pup who enjoys rubbing noses with the celebrities he meets when accompanying his parents to work, renovating his country house, and collecting wine. Hobbies include tormenting his parents with the loudest squeaky toys he can find, playing Wrestlemania Smackdown with best friend Peanut, and, of course, showing off his repertoire of tricks for his many admirers. A regular trixie + peanut model since he was a puppy, Mac can now be seen in national commercials and publications.

Neck

Sizes 24 & 28 only: (P8, p2tog) around. [— (—, —, 45, —, 55) sts]

Purl.

(P7, p2tog) around.

Size 26 only: (P6, p2tog) around. [— (—, —, —, 49, —) sts]

Purl.

(P5, p2tog) around.

All sizes: [18 (22, 26, 40, 42, 49) sts]

*K1, p1; rep from * around, ending p2tog if necessary to end round in purl. [18 (22, 26, 40, 42, 48) sts]

Continue in rib for 2 (2, 2, 4, 4, 4)″ more.

Bind off in rib.

Finishing

Weave in ends.
Block if desired.

Wyatt *sits at attention in his camo chic sweater.*

Mac *plays peek-a-boo!*

POOCH PROFILE: PEANUT

Rescued Boxer beauty and company namesake, Peanut has perfected her supermodel pout after years of practice. Infamous in her younger days for jumping the fence at the dog run, Peanut is still regularly outsmarting her parents. Sensitive, intelligent, and a tomboy at heart, Peanut's many hobbies include streaking around naked on the roof of her Manhattan apartment building, chasing squirrels in the park, counter surfing, and adding to her vast modern art collection. Seven-years-young, Peanut thrives on daily yoga sessions, bison bones, and her homemade, all-natural raw diet prepared daily by her personal chefs (aka Mom and Dad). As co-founder of trixie + peanut, Peanut now spends most of her time running the day-to-day retail operations of the business.

Cookie and Peanut prove that size doesn't matter when it comes to looking good in a bulky, warm sweater.

Chew on This!

Polo is a game that is played on horseback. The version of the game still played today originated in Punjab, India, in 1862. The horses ridden in games of polo, known as "polo ponies," require six months to a year of training. Polo ponies must learn how to stop quickly and change directions while maintaining their stride and speed.

POLO SHIRT

This preppy sweater was designed with a certain Miniature Pinscher in mind. His perky step and pointy ears inspired the stand-up collar and bold color combination. Your dog will be the hippest dog on the block in this fetching sweater.

POLO SHIRT

[THIN DOGS]

Sizes: 14 (16, 18, 20, 22, 24)

To fit chest: 14–15 (16–17, 18–19, 19–20, 20–21, 20–21)"

Yarn:
Baabajoes Wool Pak Yarns NZ 14-ply (100% wool, 8.8 oz/250 g, 310 yds/283 m), 1 skein main color (MC)
Blue Sky Alpacas Blue Sky Cotton (100% cotton; 3.8 oz/110 g; 150 yds/138 m), 1 skein stripe color (CC).

You don't need a full skein for the contrasting stripes. You can use whatever yarn you have on hand in a similar gauge. I favor the unusual mix of wool and cotton, but I also love using Wool Pak for both colors.

Wool Pak skeins are quite long, so should you decide to use it for the stripes as well, you'll have plenty left over to make another sweater in reverse colors.

Yarn Symbol:

Gauge: 14 sts and 20 rows = 4" (10 cm) in stockinette stitch.

Needles: One 16" (40 cm) circular needle size US #10 1/2 (6.5 mm) or size needed to obtain correct gauge

Other: Tapestry needle, ring markers, stitch holder, split ring markers or safety pins

14 (16, 18, 20, 22, 24)"

14 1/4 (15 1/2, 16 1/2, 17 3/4, 18 3/4, 20)"

BODY

CC, loosely cast on 34 (34, 34, 38, 38, 38) sts.

Row 1 (WS) * K1, p1; rep from *. Cut CC.

Rows 2–5: With MC, *k1, p1; rep from *.

Stripe Pattern: Work 2 rows CC and 8 rows MC. This pattern continues throughout. Cut the contrasting color yarn between stripes.

Increase for Back

Continuing in established stripe pattern,

Row 1: Knit.

Row 2: Purl.

Row 3: K1, m1, knit to last stitch, m1, k1. [36 (36, 36, 40, 40, 40) sts]

Row 4: Purl.

Rep these four rows 7 (9, 11, 11, 13, 15) more times, ending with Row 4. [50 (54, 58, 62, 66, 70) sts]

Belly

Continuing in pattern, knit across next row.

At this point your 50 (54, 58, 62, 66, 70) stitches should be wrapping around the circular needle in such a way that it will be obvious how to create the necessary tubular shape for belly. Place a marker to signify beginning of new round. Join into the round by knitting into stitches from left needle, being careful not to twist.

Knit all rounds in pattern until piece measures 13 (15, 17, 19, 21, 23)" from beginning.

Just eight weeks old and our little **Cowboy** *has already earned his stripes!*

Leg Openings

Continuing in pattern, k5 (5, 5, 7, 7, 7), bind off 5 (5, 5, 7, 7, 7) sts, knit to last 10 (10, 10, 14, 14, 14) sts, bind off 5 (5, 5, 7, 7, 7), k5 (5, 5, 7, 7, 7).

Remove marker and knit across next 5 (5, 5, 7, 7, 7) sts. Turn work.

You will now be working back and forth on the 10 (10, 10, 14, 14, 14) middle stitches.

Purl one row.

Row 1: Knit.

Row 2: Purl.

Row 3: K1, m1, k to last stitch, m1, k1.

Row 4: Purl.

Rep last four rows 3 (4, 5, 6, 7, 7) more times. [18 (20, 22, 28, 30, 30) sts]

Rep Rows 3 & 4 1 (1, 1, 2, 2, 3) times. [20 (22, 24, 32, 34, 36) sts]

Rep Row 3. [22 (24, 26, 34, 36, 38) sts]

If necessary, rep Rows 1 & 2 to align with stripe pattern of back, ending with a purl row.

Neck

Use two different colored stitch markers. Pick one color to indicate the start of a new round.

Place first marker to indicate new round, knit across stitches for back, place other marker, knit across 22 (24, 26, 34, 36, 38) chest stitches. [52 (58, 64, 68, 74, 80) sts]

Continue to knit rounds in stripe pattern until back measures 14 (16, 18, 20, 22, 24)" from beginning.

Neck and Shoulder Shaping

Round 1: *Ssk, knit to 2 sts before next marker, k2tog, slip marker. Rep from *. [48 (54, 60, 64, 70, 76) sts]

Round 2: Knit.

Rep Rounds 1 & 2 once more. [44 (50, 56, 60, 66, 72) sts]

Rep Round 1.

Bind off loosely.

COLLAR

From right and left neck decrease seams, measure 1 (1, 1, 2, 2, 2)" towards center of chest and mark with split ring marker or safety pin. Starting at left marker, right side facing, with MC, pick up 34 (38, 42, 46, 50, 54) sts around back to next marker.

Work k1, p1 rib for 3 rows, ending with a wrong side row.

Collar shaping

Row 1: K1, *p1, k1; rep from * to last stitch, p1f&b. [35 (39, 43, 47, 51, 55) sts]

Row 2: *P1, k1; rep from * to last stitch, p1f&b.

Row 3: P1, *k1, p1; rep from * last stitch, k1f&b.

Row 4: *K1, p1; rep from * to last stitch, k1f&b.

Rows 5-6: Rep Rows 1-2. [40 (44, 48, 52, 56, 60) sts]

Cut MC.

With CC, bind off in rib.

Finishing

Block. Weave in tails.

Handsome **Mac** *makes all the girls swoon in his fetching polo shirt.*

Chew on This!

Alpaca yarn is made from the fleece of the alpaca, which is a relative of the camel. Many alpacas live in South America and are often domesticated. Their fleece is long, soft, and silky. Alpaca owners generally shear their alpacas once a year, and can get up to seven pounds of wool from just one.

RIBBON DRESS

Life in New York City provides endless interactions with all types of personalities, particularly dogs. Some dogs are, without a doubt, meant to wear dresses. This pattern is for them. The addition of luxurious silk provides this alpaca yarn with a beautiful drape and shine. It is also easy to change the accompanying accent ribbon to suit the season or to freshen the look.

RIBBON DRESS

[FOR SMALL TO MEDIUM DOGS]

Sizes: 8 (10, 12, 14, 16, 18)

To fit belly: 11 1/2–12 1/2 (12 1/2–13 1/2, 13 1/2–14 1/2, 14 1/2–15 1/2, 15 1/2–16 1/2, 16 1/2–17 1/2)"

Yarn: Blue Sky Alpacas Alpaca and Silk (50% Alpaca, 50% silk; 1.75 oz / 50 g, 146 yds/ 133 m), 2 (2, 2, 3, 3, 3) skeins main color (MC), 1 skein contrasting color (CC)

Yarn Weight:

Gauge: 22 sts and 28 rows = 4" (10 cm) in stockinette stitch

Needles: One set US #4 (3.5 mm) double-pointed needles. One 16" (40 cm) circular needle size US #4 (3.5 mm) or size needed to obtain correct gauge

Other: 2 (3) yards of 1–2" wide ribbon, tapestry needle, stitch markers

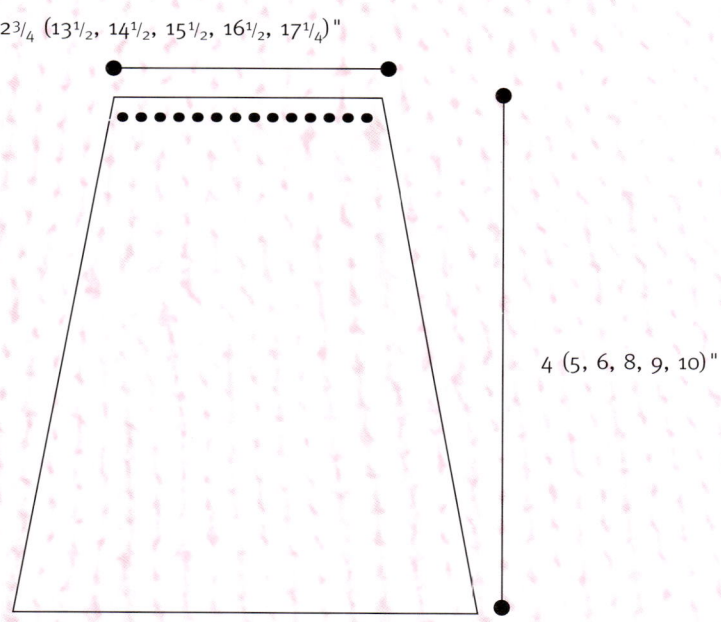

SKIRT

Picot Hem

With CC, loosely cast on 80 (90, 100, 110, 120, 130) sts.

Place marker and join for working in the round, being careful not to twist stitches.

Knit 4 rounds.

*Yo, k2tog, rep from * around.

Knit 3 rounds.

Next round: With right needle, pick up first loop from cast on edge and place it on left needle, k2tog. Continue in this way across all stitches. Each loop you pick up should be directly below the stitch it will be knitted with in order to maintain an even hem. Cut CC.

Skirt Shaping

With MC, knit 8 rounds.

Decrease Round 1:

*K14 (16, 18, 20, 22, 24), k2tog; rep from *.
[75 (85, 95, 105, 115, 125) sts]

Knit 8 rounds

Decrease Round 2:

*K13 (15, 17, 19, 21, 23), k2tog; rep from *.
[70 (80, 90, 100, 110, 120) sts]

Knit 8 rounds.

Kayla *strikes her "Don't hate me because I'm beautiful" pose.*

POOCH PROFILE: KAYLA

Glamorous Kayla is a four-legged diva-in-training. A spirited year-old Boston Terrier, Kayla is a small dog with a big personality. Always remembered for her impressive bunny rabbit impersonation, Kayla possesses unparalleled energy and endurance. She has been known to bark for three hours straight (a diva must let her presence be known!). Kayla enjoys rides in the elevator of her luxury high-rise building without parental supervision, of course! Amazingly adept at spotting fake designer handbags, Kayla, with the help of her generous parents, has amassed a much-envied wardrobe. Born into NYC's in-crowd, Kayla is often spotted hanging out with the beautiful people at all the important social events.

Sizes 10–18 only:
* K - (14, 16, 18, 20, 22), k2tog; rep from *.
Knit 8 rounds.

Sizes 12–18 only:
* K - (-, 15, 17, 19, 21), k2tog; rep from *.
Knit 8 rounds.

Sizes 14–18 only:
* K - (-, -, 16, 18, 20), k2tog; rep from *.
Knit 8 rounds.

Sizes 16–18 only:
* K - (-, -, -, 17, 19) k2tog; rep from *.
Knit 8 rounds.

Size 18 only:
*- (-, -, -, -, 18), k2tog; rep from *.
Knit 8 rounds.

All Sizes: [70 (85, 80, 85, 90, 95) sts]

Knit all rounds until piece measures 4 (5, 6, 8, 9, 10)" to picot edge.

Eyelet Round

Sizes 8, 12 & 16: K2, *yo, k2tog, k3; rep from * to last 3 sts, yo, k2tog, k1.

Sizes 10, 14 & 18: K4, *yo, k2tog, k3; rep from * to last stitch, k1.

All Sizes: Knit all rounds for 1" more.

SLEEVES

K18 (19, 20, 21, 22, 24), bind off 8 (8, 8, 12, 12, 12) sts, k18 (21, 24, 19, 22, 23), bind off 8 (8, 8, 12, 12, 12) sts, knit to end of round.

K18 (19, 20, 21, 22, 24), pm, cast on 16 (16, 16, 24, 24, 24) sts, pm, k18 (19, 20, 21, 22, 24), pm, cast on 16 (16, 16, 24, 24, 24), pm, knit to end of round.

Use different colored stitch markers than the one used to indicate new rounds.

Knit 6 rounds.

*Knit to 2 sts before next marker, k2tog, ssk, rep from *.

Knit 1 round.

Rep last two rounds 3 (3, 3, 5, 5, 5) more times, switching to double pointed needles when necessary. [54 (57, 60, 63, 66, 72) sts]

Neck

Knit 5 rounds. Cut MC.

With CC, knit 4 rounds.

Sizes 10 & 14 only: K1, *yo, k2tog; rep from *.

Other sizes: *Yo, k2tog, rep from *.

Knit 3 rounds.

Bind off.

Finishing

Block. Fold picot edge at neck and sew to inside. Weave in ends.

Starting at middle back, weave ribbon through eyelets. Try sweater on dog and tie ribbon into a bow. Cut any excess ribbon.

Remove ribbon to wash.

Chew on This!

To be hung correctly, a dart board must be mounted so that the bull's eye is exactly 5' 7" from the floor. A regulation dartboard is divided into 20 areas, all of the same size, each shaped like a wedge of a pie. By hitting a bull's eye, a player can earn 25 points. A double bull's eye is worth 50 points!

BULL'S EYE

This sweater is inspired by the graphic quality of archery targets. These sweaters were made with a combination of two colors, rather than the traditional yellow, red, blue, black, and white. Harrisville Designs creates a wonderful line of pure wool yarns that illuminate traditional textures with twists of fresh color. Koigu Kersti is absolutely one of the best hand-dyed yarns. When picking your color combination for this sweater, start with Harrisville and inspect the skein for color cues for a contrasting color. There are often subtle traces of that perfect pairing, which Koigu colors are sure to satisfy.

BULL'S EYE

[PATTERN ADJUSTABLE TO SUIT MOST DOGS]

Sizes: 14 (20, 28)

To fit belly: 14–20 (20–28, 28+)"
The belly strap makes this pattern adjustable.

Yarn: Harrisville Highland Style (100% pure virgin wool, 3.5 oz/100 g, 200 yds/ 183 m), 1 skein dark color (MC)
Koigu Kersti Merino Crepe (100% merino wool, 1.75 oz/50 g, 114 yds/100 m), 1 (1, 2) skeins light color (CC)

Yarn Weight:

Gauge: 20 sts and 24 rounds = 4" (10 cm) in stockinette stitch

Needles: One 24" (60 cm) circular needle size US #7 (4.5 mm), one 16" (40 cm) circular needle size US #7 (4.5 mm), one set double-pointed needles size US #7 (4.5 mm), or size needed to obtain correct gauge

Other: Two 3/4" buttons, crochet hook size G-6 (4 mm), tapestry needle, safety pins or split ring markers

This pattern is an adaptation of Elizabeth Zimmerman's Pi shawl.

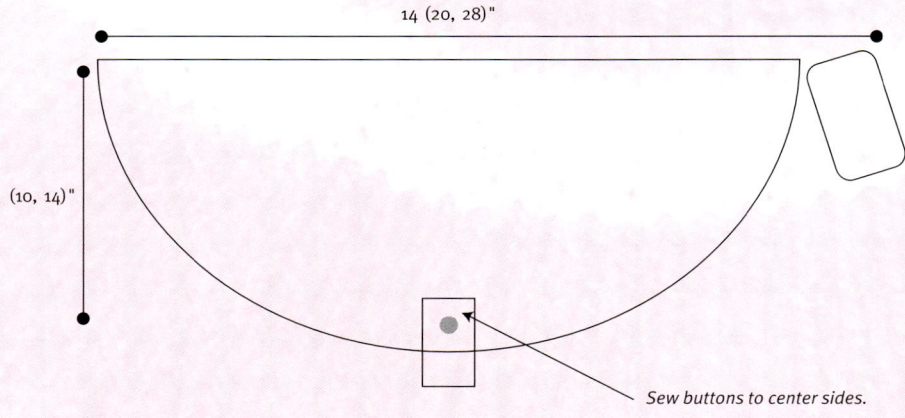

Sew buttons to center sides.

BODY

Crochet Cast-On

Using crochet cast-on method, cast on 9 sts. Transfer stitches onto three double pointed needles placing 3 sts on each needle.

Knit one round. Before knitting next round, place a safety pin or split ring marker into work to mark beginning of round.

Switch to circular needles when necessary.

Dapper dog **Lucy** *is all smiles!*

Increase Round: Knit into front and back of each stitch. [18 sts]

Knit 3 rounds.

Work Increase Round [36 sts]

With CC, knit 6 rounds

Work Increase Round. [72 sts]

With MC, knit 12 rounds.

Work Increase Round. [144 sts]

With CC, knit 6 rounds.

*P1, sl1; rep from *.

(Skip ahead to †† for size 14)

With MC, knit 12 rounds.

*P1, sl1; rep from *.

With CC, knit 6 rounds.

Work Increase Round. [288 sts]

(Skip ahead to †† for size 20)

With MC, knit 12 rounds.

Next round: *P1, sl1; rep from *.

With CC, knit 6 rounds.

*P1, sl1; rep from *.

†† With MC, knit 6 rounds.

Purl 5 rounds.

Bind off 120 (258, 252) sts in purl. [24 (30, 36) sts remain]

Neck

Using 16″ circular or double-pointed needles, purl across 24 (30, 36) sts, cast on 24 (30, 36) sts.

Place marker and join into round being careful not to twist stitches.

Purl 10 (15, 20) rounds.

With CC, knit 10 rounds.

Bind off loosely in knit.

Finishing

At first this sweater will look like a strange ruffled doily. In order to achieve a nice flat shape, you must block it. Give the sweater

a good soak in cold water and remove excess water by rolling in a towel. Pin opposite sides of the circle first and continue around the outside. Don't be afraid to stretch your work or pin and re-pin to make the circle even. Leave the contrasting color band at neck unblocked to allow it to roll.

Sew Buttons

See diagram for placement of buttons. Use yarn to sew both buttons into place.

Strap

Once dry, try the sweater on your dog. Measure belly from button to button to determine length of strap. Add one inch to this measurement and work as follows:

With MC, cast on 12 sts.

Knit 6 rows.

Make Button Hole: K5, bind off 2 sts, knit to end.

K5, cast on 2 sts, knit to end.

Work even until strap is 1″ shorter than desired length.

Make a second buttonhole.

Knit 6 rows.

Bind off. Weave in tails.

A double bull's eye for **Cookie***!*

Chew on This!

Herringbone is also a term used in skiing. It describes a method of going up a slope. The skier sets his or her skis in a form that resembles a V while placing his or her weight on the inside edges. The skis are moved forward in turns, and the skier uses his or her poles for both support and propulsion.

HERRINGBONE JACKET

This particular herringbone variation may be our favorite stitch pattern. Handsome and sophisticated, the stitches end up crossing to produce a dense, almost woven texture. Since it's hard to pick only one of the countless Koigu colors, use two, and don't be afraid to be daring in your color choices!

HERRINGBONE JACKET

[SMALL TO MEDIUM DOGS WITH BIGGER CHESTS]

Sizes: 10 (12, 14, 16, 18)

To fit chest: 14–16 (16–18, 18–20, 20–22, 22–24)"

Yarn: Koigu KPM Semi Solids (100% Merino Wool, 1.75 oz/50 g, 75 yds/ 160 m), 2 (2, 3, 3, 4) skeins each of two colors (A) and (B).
NOTE: Yarn is used double throughout.

Yarn Weight:

Gauge: 30 sts and 22 rows = 4" in Herringbone Pattern Stitch with yarn used double. Note: A single strand of KPM yarn has a gauge of 28 sts = 4" (10 cm) on US #3 (3.25 mm) needles

Needles: One pair straight needle size US #9 (5.5 mm), or size needed to obtain correct gauge

Other: 5 (7, 9, 11, 13)" strip of sewable Velcro, tapestry needle, crochet hook to pick up stitches, split ring markers or safety pins

This complex looking stitch is pretty straightforward, but it does take a little practice to feel confident. I suggest making a generous gauge swatch in order to try it out.

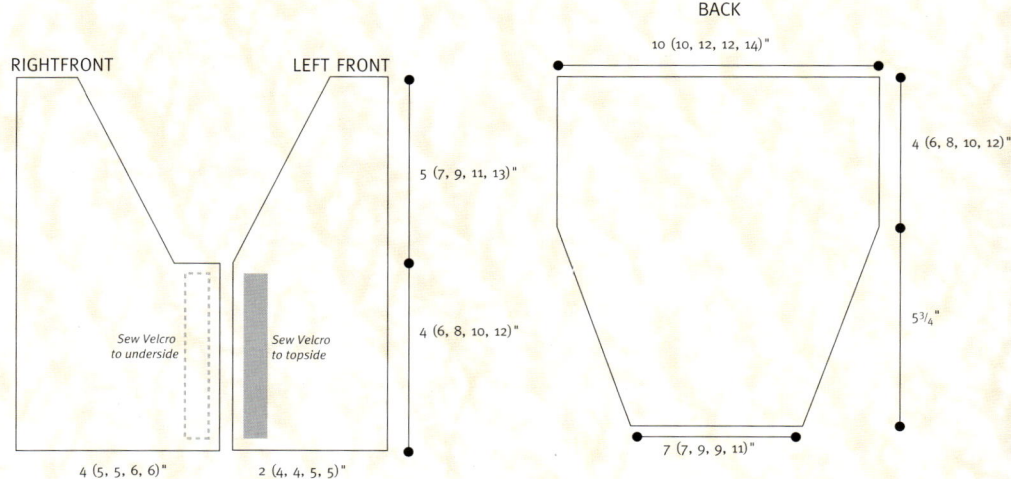

At this point, place a split ring marker on left and right edges of piece. You will sew the front pieces to this point later.

Continue in pattern until piece measures 10 (12, 14, 16, 18)″ from beginning. Bind off in pattern.

Right side facing, on bound-off edge measure 3″ toward center from each side edge and place markers. Later you will use these markers to sew shoulder seams.

HERRINGBONE STITCH (any number of sts)

Knit Pattern Row: *K2togtbl and slip only the first stitch onto right needle, leaving second stitch on left needle; rep from * to last stitch, k1.

Purl Pattern Row: *P2tog and slip only the first stitch off onto right needle, leaving second stitch on left needle; rep from * to last stitch, p1.

Rep these 2 rows.

Seed Stitch (odd number of sts)

Row 1: K1, *p1, k1; rep from *.

Rep Row 1.

BACK

Holding together one strand of each color, cast on 52 (52, 66, 66, 82) sts.

Row 1 (WS): Purl Pattern Row.

Row 2: Knit Pattern Row.

Row 3: Purl Pattern to last stitch, p1f&b.

Row 4: Knit Pattern to last stitch, k1f&b.

Rep these four rows 3 more times. [60 (60, 74, 74, 80) sts]

Rep Rows 3 & 4 eight times. [76 (76, 90, 90, 106) sts]

Perfect gentleman **Chico Suave** *is dressed to impress.*

RIGHT FRONT

Cast on 30 (38, 38, 45, 45) sts.

Work in Herringbone Pattern until piece measures 4 (6, 8, 10, 12)" ending with a Purl Pattern Row.

Bind off 8 sts at beginning of next row. Continue in Herringbone Pattern across remaining stitches.

Decrease for neck

Decreasing in Herringbone Stitch requires a slightly different approach than your normal knitting decrease. I find the easiest and most attractive way to decrease is at the end of a row. This way the decreased stitch will virtually disappear and remain consistent to the pattern. Here's how you do it:

Knit row decrease: Work Herringbone Pattern to last 2 sts, k2togtbl.

Purl row decrease: Work Herringbone Pattern to last 2 sts, p2tog.

It really is this simple! Now just follow the directions for your size.

Continuing in pattern, work as follows:

Sizes 10 & 12 only: Decrease at end of *every* Purl Pattern Row 11 (15, -, -, -) times.

Sizes 14 & 16 only: Decrease at the end of *every other* Purl Pattern Row - (-, 11, 13, -) times.

Size 18 only: Decrease at the end of *every third* Purl Pattern Row – (-, -, -, 11) times.

All sizes: [11 (15, 19, 24, 26) sts]

Work even in pattern until piece measures 9 (13, 17, 21, 25)" from beginning.

Bind off in pattern.

LEFT FRONT

Cast on 22 (30, 30, 37, 37) sts.

Work in pattern until piece measures 4 (6, 8, 10, 12)" from beginning, ending with a Knit Pattern Row.

Continuing in pattern, work as follows:

Sizes 10 & 12 only: Decrease at end of *every* Knit Pattern Row 11 (15, -, -, -) times.

Sizes 14 & 16 only: Decrease at the end of *every other* Knit Pattern Row - (-, 11, 13, -) times.

Size 18 only: Decrease at the end of *every third* Knit Pattern Row – (-, -, -, 11) times.

All sizes: [11 (15, 19, 24, 26) sts]

Work even in pattern until piece measures 9 (13, 17, 21, 25)" from beginning.

Bind off in pattern.

Finishing

Block pieces.

Because seams can be tricky to hide in this stitch, I've decided to make them obvious along the sides. You could use any method you want.

With wrong sides together, match bottom of Right Front to marker on side of Back. Right side facing, single crochet pieces together.

Rep for Left Front.

Match outside edge of Left Front to corresponding marker on Back. Sew shoulder seam.

Rep for right shoulder seam.

Collar

Right side facing, beginning at end of bound-off stitches on Right Front, use crochet hook to pick up 57 (77, 97, 125, 157) sts along shaped Right Front edge, across back and along shaped Left Front edge.

Work in Seed Stitch for 9 (9, 11, 11, 13) rows. (See page 83 for Seed Stitch.)

With two strands of the same color, work Seed Stitch for 2 rows.

Bind off in Seed Stitch. Sew Velcro on front edges (see diagram).

POOCH PROFILE: DIXIE

Miss Dixie Gallant is a darling two-year-old Southern beauty who is known for her magnificent profile and graceful, svelte figure. Born and raised in Georgia, Dixie now calls New York City her home. Always courteous, well-mannered, and delightfully diplomatic, Dixie is a "pup"licist at her mom's PR firm, where she effortlessly charms clients, skillfully manages million dollar accounts, and frequently hobnobs with celebrities. When not acquiring more designer toys to add to her exquisite collection, Dixie can often be seen sipping sweet iced tea while sunbathing on her Gramercy Park terrace with her favorite tune, "Georgia On My Mind," playing on her vintage record player.

Chew on This!

The term argyle refers to a criss-crossed diamond knitting pattern that was first seen and worn in Scotland. Novelist Sir Walter Scott is partially responsible for opening the world's eyes to argyle when he made reference to the pattern in one of his works. Enormously popular in the 1920s, argyle is still hotter than ever!

ARGYLE SWEATER

We're always on the lookout for great argyle patterns. Argyle sweaters are both classic and hip, and they never go out of style! Working with a fuzzy yarn like angora makes this sweater extra adorable.

ARGYLE SWEATER

[FITS MOST DOGS]

Sizes: 8 (12, 16, 20)

To fit chest: 10–12 (14–16, 18–20, 22–24)" Chest width is not easily changed due to color pattern.

Yarn: Classic Elite Lush (50% wool, 50% angora, 1.75 oz/50 g, 124 yds/113 m), 1 (1, 2, 3) skeins main color (MC), 1 skein each diamond color (A) and bold color (B)

Yarn Weight:

Gauge: 18 sts and 24 rows = 4" (10 cm) in Argyle Pattern

Needles:
One 16" (40 cm) US #8 (5 mm) circular needle; one set US #8 (5 mm) double-pointed needles, or size needed to obtain correct gauge
Sizes 16 & 20 only: one 20" (50 cm) US #8 (5 mm) circular needle

Other: Tapestry needle, crochet hook to pick up stitches, stitch markers

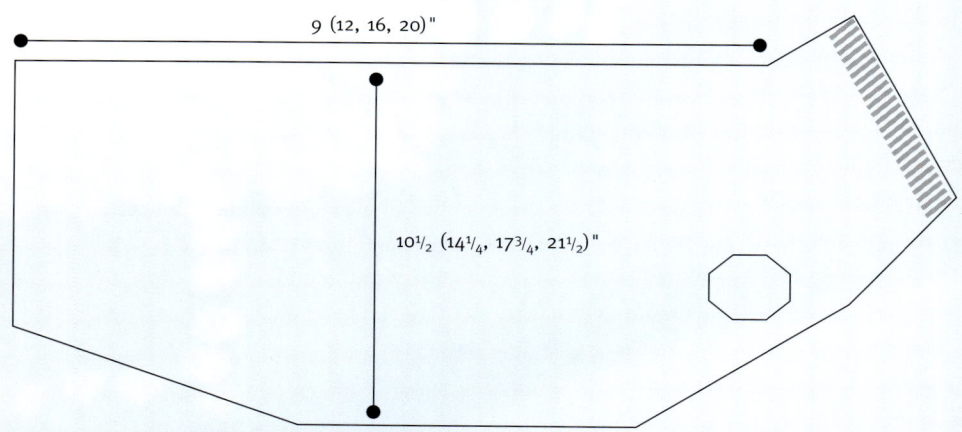

BACK

With longer needle and B, cast on 24 (36, 40, 50) sts.

Row 1 (RS): *K1, p1; rep from * across.

Rows 2–6: Rep Row 1. Cut B.

Increase for belly

Row 1: With MC, k1, m1, k to last 2 sts, m1, k2. [26 (38, 42, 52) sts]

Row 2: Purl.

Rep these two rows 11 (13, 19, 22) more times. [48 (64, 80, 96) sts]

Work even until piece measures 5 1/2 (8, 10 3/4, 13 1/2)" from beginning, ending with a wrong side row.

Work color chart over next 17 rows.

With MC, work even 1 row. Do not turn at end of row, but place marker and begin working in rounds. Work in the round for 1/2".

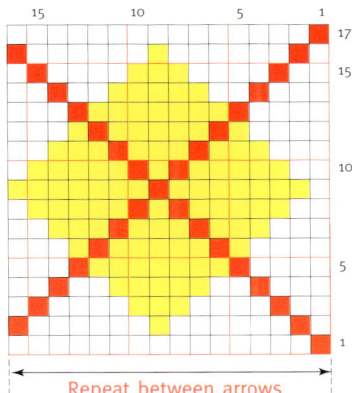

Repeat between arrows

The combination of colored diamonds and lines that produce an argyle pattern is actually more intimidating than it is difficult. Argyle diamonds are knit using the intarsia method—separate balls of each of the two colors. Ignore the bold color lines until the knitting is complete, then duplicate stitch them as indicated in the chart.

Diamonds can be a boy's best friend, too!

Mac lays down the fashion law.

Change to smaller circular needle or double-pointed needles as necessary.

Rep these two rounds 2 (3, 4, 5) more times. [45 (68, 84, 100) sts]

Knit one round.

Neck Opening

Rounds 1–7: *K1, p1; rep from *.

Cut MC.

Rounds 8–9: With B, *k1, p1; rep from *.

Bind off loosely in rib.

Leg Cuffs

With B, pick up 18 (24, 28, 30) sts around leg opening and place on double pointed needles.

Rounds 1–5: *K1, p1; rep from *.

Bind off in rib.

Finishing

This sweater will benefit from a good blocking. This yarn will felt quite easily, so treat it carefully.

Sew center seam. Weave in tails.

Leg Openings

K4 (5, 6, 7), bind off 5 (6, 7, 8) sts, knit to last 9 (11, 13, 15) sts, bind off 5 (6, 7, 8) sts, knit to end.

When placing markers for armhole decreases, use a different color than that used to indicate the start of new round.

K4 (5, 6, 7), pm, cast on 8 (12, 14, 16) sts, pm, knit to next leg opening, pm, cast on 8 (12, 14, 16) sts, pm, k4 (5, 6, 7). [54 (76, 94, 112) sts]

On the leg openings, it is correct to cast on more stitches than you bind off. This widens the chest a little bit.

Work even until piece measures 9 (12, 16, 20)" from beginning.

* Knit to 2 sts before marker, k2tog, slip marker, ssk; rep from *.

Knit one round.

POOCH PROFILE: FINNEGAN

Irish-born, fun-loving Finnegan is an extraordinary Yorkshire Terrier who has grown to a statuesque fifteen pounds, leading many to believe he may actually be part billy goat! Like his size, Finnegan, known as "Finnie" to his peers, has an oversized personality. He possesses a kind heart and generous love for all things. Friendly, gentle, and always well-dressed, Finnegan loves greeting his favorite doorman each morning, accompanying his mom to the salon for manis/pedis, and spending time in the country with his Maltese cousin Sophie. Finnie spends his days in New York City's Washington Square Park, charming the NYU coeds at the dog run and surprising the stiff competition on the chess boards.

Chew on This!

Some animals look as if they are wearing hoods even when they're not! The European hooded crow has a gray body and a black head. The North Atlantic hooded seal has a large hoodlike sac on the front of its head that it inflates when it feels threatened. The cobra uses its hood to warn other animals of an impending attack.

HOODIE

Dogs must be jealous of our hoodies. A hoodie is, after all, one of the most perfect articles of clothing ever designed. Warm, soft, snug, and oversized—your little friend will want to wear this sweater all the time! Made with supersoft cotton, this sweater will fit your dog loosely—without ever getting too itchy or heavy. And who knows, making this for your pup might even inspire a new jogging regimen for the two of you!

HOODIE

[OVERSIZED TO FIT SMALL TO LARGE DOGS IN ALL SHAPES]

Sizes: 12 (14, 16, 18, 20, 22, 24)

To fit chest: Take measurement

Yarn: Blue Sky Alpacas Blue Sky Cotton (100% cotton; 3.9 oz/110 g, 150 yds/138 m), 2 (2, 3, 3, 4, 4, 4, 5) skeins

Yarn Weight:

Gauge: 16 sts and 20 rows = 4" (10 cm)

Needles: One pair straight needles size US #9 (5.5 mm) or size needed to obtain correct gauge

Other: 8 (9, 11, 12, 14, 14, 16)" separating zipper, one 36–40" shoelace for hood tie, tapestry needle, ring markers, stitch holder, sewing needle and matching thread. (You may need to look on the Internet for custom-sized zippers if the sewing stores in your area have limited zipper supplies.)

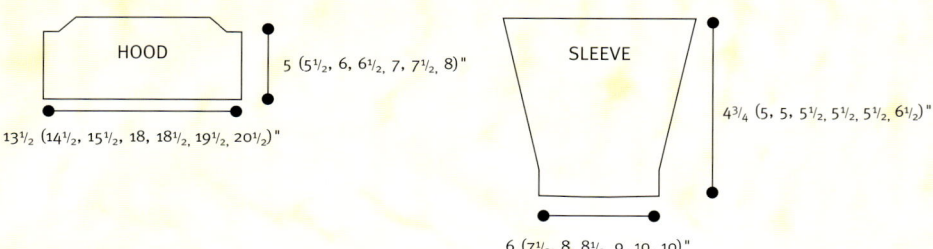

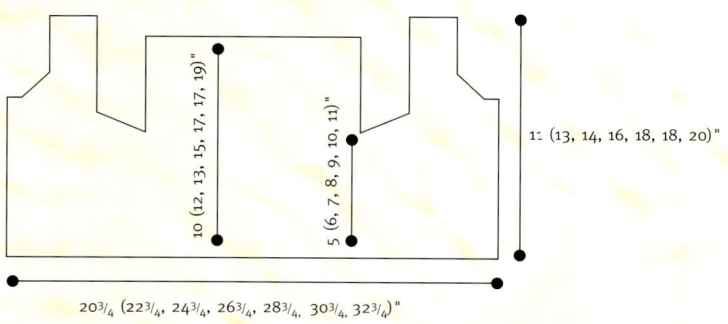

BODY

The body and sides of this sweater are knit in one piece to the armhole.

Cast on 83 (91, 99, 107, 115, 123, 131) sts.

Row 1 (RS): P4, * k1, p1, rep from * to last 5 sts, k1, p4.

Row 2: K4, *p1, k1, rep from * to last 5 sts, p1, k4.

Rep these two rows until piece measures 1 (1, 1, 1, 2, 2, 2)" ending with a wrong side row.

Next row (RS): P4, knit to last 4 sts, p4.

Next row: K4, purl to last 4 sts, k4.

Work even, keeping first and last 4 sts in reverse stockinette stitch, until piece measures 5 (6, 7, 8, 9, 10, 11)" from beginning, ending with a wrong side row.

RIGHT FRONT

P4, k24 (26, 28, 30, 32, 34, 36), turn.

You will now be working on Right Front stitches only. If desired, place remaining stitches on a stitch holder until you need them.

Purl to last 4 sts, k4.

Decrease for Leg Opening

Row 1: P4, knit to last 4 sts, k2tog, k2.

Row 2: Purl to last 4 sts, k4.

Rep last two rows 3 (3, 5, 5, 7, 7, 7) more times. [20 (22, 22, 24, 24, 26, 28) sts]

Work even until Right Front measures 8 (9, 11, 12, 14, 14, 16)" from beginning, ending with a wrong side row.

Lucy's *feelin' good in the 'hood.*

Neck

Bind off 4 sts, knit to end.

Purl one row.

K2, ssk, knit to end.

Purl one row.

Rep last two rows 3 (5, 5, 5, 5, 7, 7) more times. [12 (12, 12, 14, 14, 14, 16) sts]

Work even until Right Front measures 11 (13, 14, 16, 18, 18, 20)" from beginning.

Bind off.

BACK

Right side facing, join yarn at back, k35 (39, 43, 47, 51, 55, 59).

Work even in stockinette stitch until Back measures 10 (12, 13, 15, 17, 17, 19)" from beginning, ending with a wrong side row.

Bind off.

LEFT FRONT

Right side facing, join yarn to at left front, knit to last 4 sts, p4.

K4, purl to end.

K2, ssk, knit to end.

K4, purl to end.

Repeat last two rows 3 (3, 5, 5, 7, 7, 7) more times. [20 (22, 22, 24, 24, 26, 28) sts]

Work even until Left Front measures 8 (9, 11, 12, 14, 14, 16)" from beginning, ending with a right side row.

Neck

Bind off 4 sts, purl to end.

Knit to last 4 sts, k2tog, k2.

Purl one row.

Replast two rows 3 (5, 5, 5, 5, 7, 7) more times. [12 (12, 12, 14, 14, 14, 16) sts]

Work even until Left Front measures 11 (13, 14, 16, 18, 18, 20)" from beginning.

Bind off.

SLEEVES (make two)

Cast on 24 (30, 32, 34, 36, 40, 40) sts.

Row 1: *K1, p1; rep from *.

Rep Row 1 until piece measures 3" from beginning, ending with a wrong side row.

There's more than one stylin' dog in this 'hood!

Sleeve Increase

Row 1: K2, m1, k to last 2 stitches, m1, k2. [26 (32, 34, 36, 38, 42, 42) sts]

Row 2: Purl.

Rep last two rows 11 (12, 12, 13, 13, 13, 15) more times. [48 (56, 58, 62, 64, 68, 72) sts]

Bind off.

Finishing

Block pieces.

Using mattress stitch, sew sleeve to leghole, with sleeve seam on top.

Sew shoulder seam from neck edge out to leg cuff. Fasten off. Repeat for other leg.

Weave in ends.

Zipper

Carefully pin zipper into place, making sure to keep knitting flat.

Backstitch zipper in place.

It may be helpful to sew the zipper twice, once along the edge to make it lay flat and once pretty close to the teeth, so it will withstand more pulling. If you think you're not a good sewer, don't worry. Messy stitches work just as well as neat ones. Just be sure to keep them away from the zipper's mechanics, or else it won't work!

HOOD

With crochet hook, right side facing, starting at beginning of right neck shaping, pick up and knit 54 (58, 62, 72, 74, 78, 82) stitches around neck edge.

Row 1 (WS): Purl to end, cast on 5 sts. [59 (63, 67, 77, 79, 83, 87) sts]

Row 2: K4, sl1, knit to end, cast on 5 sts. [64 (68, 72, 82, 84, 88, 92) sts]

Row 3: Purl.

Row 4: K4, sl1, knit to last 5 sts, sl1, k4.

Repeat last two rows until hood measures 5 (5½, 6, 6½, 7, 7½, 8)" ending with a wrong side row.

Shape Hood

Row 1: K4, sl1, k 27 (29, 31, 36, 37, 39, 41), pm, knit to last 5 sts, sl1, k4.

Row 2: Purl.

Row 3: K4, s1, knit to 2 sts before marker, k2tog, ssk, knit to last 5 sts, sl1, k4.

Row 4: Purl.

Repeat last two rows 2 more times.

Bind off.

Sew top of hood seam and inside hood casing.

Use safety pin to thread shoelace through hood casing.

Weave in ends.

POOCH PROFILE: JOHNNY

Gorgeous guy Johnny Walker Black is a precocious Lab puppy. A mere eight weeks old when he posed for this picture, Johnny stops NYC traffic whenever he steps out with his handsome father, Ty, and debonair uncle Justin, both magnificent Labrador Retrievers. Johnny is squishy, squeezable, and absolutely lovable, and no one can resist his charms—even his dog-trainer mom, who is sure that Johnny will grow up to be a Best-in-Breed champion. Proving that the pup doesn't stray far from the pack, Johnny loves playing with children, enjoys long car rides, has a genius IQ of 132, and is especially fond of classical music. A second generation trixie + peanut model, Johnny is currently concentrating on his acting career and can often be seen signing autographs in the park.

Chew on This!

Patchwork pieces have been crafted—and admired!—since the earliest times. Ancient Buddhists created patchworks out of square and rectangular pieces of silk. Some monks even constructed their own habits out of patchwork in order to signify their commitment to poverty.

PATCHWORK BLANKET

This is the perfect patchwork blanket for your dog. Maybe now he or she will leave *yours* alone! We love this pattern because you can make it as easy or as difficult as you want. We encourage you to take a risk and be as imaginative as possible in your stitch and color selections. Let your creativity take charge!

PATCHWORK BLANKET
[ALL DOGS]

Size: 36" x 36"

Yarn: Lorna's Laces Shepherd Bulky (100% Superwash wool, 4 oz/ 113 g, 140 yds/ 128 m), 2 skeins of each of the five colors. You will have leftover yarn. If you'd like, use six colors instead which will require only one skein per color.

Yarn Weight:

Gauge: 16 sts = 4" (10 cm) in stockinette stitch. Gauge is not terribly important in this pattern, and it will vary according to stitch pattern. Use this as a guide.

Needles: One pair straight needles size US #9 (5.5 mm) or size needed to obtain correct gauge

Other: Tapestry needle, blocking pins

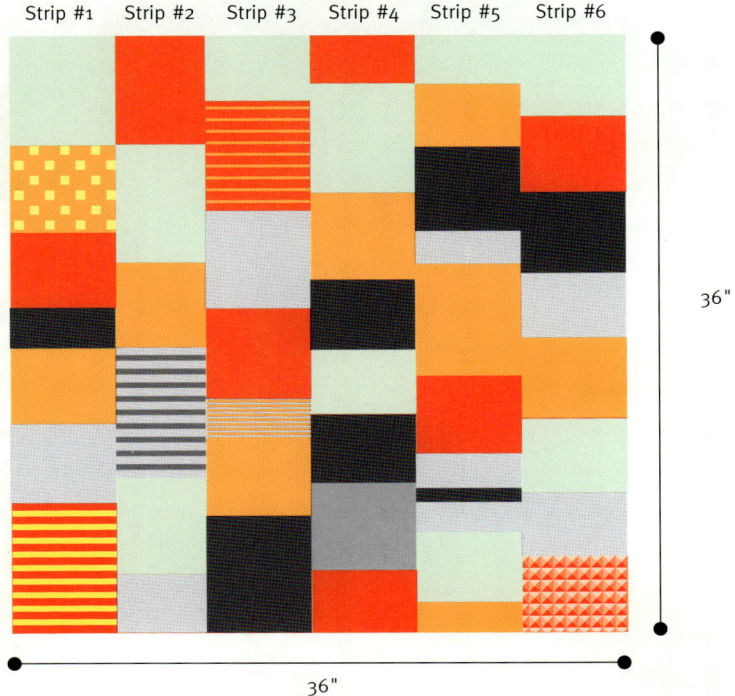

STRIP (Make 6)

Cast on 20 or 21 sts.

Each stitch pattern requires a specific number of stitches, so cast on the number required for your first pattern. Adding one stitch here and there between stitch patterns is fine and will only add to the patchwork effect.

Work in desired stitch patterns and colors until strip measures 36".

Bind off.

When changing colors, do so on the wrong side by purling one row in the new color. You will then be able to commence a new stitch pattern with a clean line between blocks.

Finishing

Block individual strips to match each other in length. Use mattress stitch to sew strips together. If necessary, block again as a whole.

SOME OF OUR FAVORITE STITCH PATTERNS

Patterns for 20 Stitches

Seed Stitch

Row 1 (RS): *K1, p1; rep from *.

Row 2: *P1, K1; rep from *.

Rep Rows 1 & 2.

2 x 2 Rib

Row 1: * K2, p2, rep from *.

Rep Row 1.

Oblique Rib

Row 1 (RS): *K2, p2; rep from *.

Row 2: K1, *p2, k2; rep from * to last 3 sts, p2, k1.

Row 3: *P2, k2; rep from *.

Row 4: P1, *k2, p2; rep from * to last 3 sts, k2, p1.

Rep Rows 1–4.

Mac is chilling out without the chills!

2 x 2 Check

Row 1 (RS): *K2, p2; rep from *.
Row 2: *K2, p2; rep from *.
Rows 3 & 4: *P2, k2; rep from *.
Row 4: *P2, k2; rep from *.
Rep Rows 1–4.

Eyelets

Row 1 (RS): Knit.
Row 2: Purl.
Row 3: K2, * yo, k2tog, k1; rep from *.
Row 4: Purl.
Rep Rows 1–4.

4 x 4 Check

Rows 1 and 3 (RS): P4, *k4, p4; rep from *.
Rows 2 and 4: K4, *P4, k4; rep from *.
Row 3: As Row 1.
Row 4: As Row 2.
Rows 5 & 7: K4, *p4, k4; rep from *.
Rows 6 & 8: P4, *k4, p4; rep from *.
Row 7: As Row 5.
Row 8: As Row 6.
Rep Rows 1–8.

1 x 1 Rib

Row 1: *K1, p1; rep from *.
Rep Row 1.

Patterns for 21 Stitches

Woven Stitch

Row 1 (RS): K1,*yf, sl1, yb, k1; rep from *.
Row 2: Purl.
Row 3: K2, *yf, sl1, yb, k1; rep from * to last stitch, k1.
Row 4: Purl.
Rep Rows 1–4.

Two-Color Woven Stitch

Work as for Woven Stitch in colors as follows:
Rows 1 & 2: With Color A.
Rows 3 & 4: With Color B.

Tweed Stitch

Row 1(RS): K1, *yf, sl1 purlwise, yb, k1; rep from *.
Row 2: P2, *yb, sl1 purlwise, yf, p1; rep from * to last stitch, p1.
Rep Rows 1 & 2.

Two dogs are more fun than one!

Rice Stitch

Row 1 (RS): P1, *k1tbl, p1; rep from *.

Row 2: Knit.

Rep Rows 1 & 2.

Seed Stitch

Row 1 (RS): K1, *p1, k1; rep from *.

Rep Row 1.

Mock Ribbing

Row 1 (RS): K1, *p1, k1; rep from *

Row 2: P1, * sl1 purlwise with yarn in front, p1; rep from *.

Rep Rows 1 & 2.

Basket Rib

Row 1 (RS): Knit.

Row 2: Purl.

Row 3: K1, *sl1 purlwise, k1; rep from *.

Row 4: K1, *yf, sl1 purlwise, yb, k1; rep from *.

Rep Rows 1–4.

Dot Stitch

Row 1 (RS): P1, *k3, p1; rep from *.

Row 2 and all even rows: Purl.

Row 3: Knit.

Row 5: K2, p1, * k3, p1; rep from * to last 2 sts, k2.

Row 7: Knit.

Row 8: Purl.

Rep Rows 1–8.

Eiffel Tower Stitch

Row 1 (RS): P4, *yo, p2tog, p2; rep from * to last stitch, p1.

Row 2: K4, *p1, k3; rep from * to last stitch, k1.

Row 3: P4, *k1, p3; rep from * to last stitch, p1.

Rep Rows 2 & 3 two more times.

Row 8: Knit.

Row 9: P2, *yo, p2tog, p2; rep from * to last 3 sts, yo, p2tog, p1.

Row 10: K2, * p1, k3; rep from * to last 3 sts, p1, k2.

Row 11: P2, *k1, p3; rep from * to last 3 sts, k1, p2.

Rep Rows 10 & 11 two more times.

Row 16: Knit.

Rep Rows 1–16.

Moss Slip Stitch

Row 1 (RS): K1, *sl1 purlwise with yarn in back, k1; rep from *.

Row 2: K1, *yf, sl1 purlwise, yb, k1; rep from *.

Row 3: K2, *sl1 purlwise with yarn in back, k1; rep from * to last stitch, k1.

Row 4: K2, *yf, sl1 purlwise, yb, k1; rep from * to last stitch, k1.

Rep Rows 1–4.

Two-Color Moss Slip Stitch

Work as for Moss Slip Stitch as follows:

Rows 1 & 2: With Color A.

Rows 3 & 4: With Color B.

POOCH PROFILE: COOKIE

Cookie, an adorable one-year-old Brussels Griffon, charms the fur off every creature she meets! Adopted at nine months old, Cookie overcame a severe eye injury to become one of the most sought after four-legged supermodels. Known for her trademark runway strut, Cookies lives the fabulous life of a pampered pooch possessing a sensational wardrobe and a stunning collection of jewelry. She even has her own fan club! When not teasing her big sister Peanut, Cookie spends her time flirting with boys, perfecting posh poses in the mirror, and designing her signature fragrance and clothing line exclusively for trixie + peanut.

Patterns for Any Number of Stitches

Garter Stitch

All Rows: Knit.

Garter Stitch Stripe

Rows 1 & 2: With Color A, knit.

Rows 3 & 4: With Color B, knit.

Rep Rows 1–4.

Garter Stitch Ridges

Rows 1 & 3 (RS): Knit.

Rows 2 & 4: Purl.

Purl 6 rows.

Rep these 10 rows.

Stockinette Stitch

Row 1 (RS): Knit.

Row 2: Purl.

Rep Rows 1 & 2.

Stockinette Stitch Stripe

Work as for Stockinette Stitch as follows:

Rows 1 & 2: With Color A.

Rows 3 & 4: With Color B.

Rep Rows 1–4.

Reverse Stockinette Stitch

Row 1 (RS): Purl.

Row 2: Knit.

Rep Rows 1 & 2.

Reverse Stockinette Stitch Stripe

Work as for Reverse Stockinette Stitch as follows:

Rows 1 & 2: With Color A.

Rows 3 & 4: With Color B.

Rep Rows 1–4.

FINISHING/CARE: BLOCKING

Blocking is a very important step that gives a polished look to your work. It is especially important when working with cotton. You'll also find that with yarns like angora and mohair, blocking with water allows them to bloom, accentuating their soft nature. These are three recommended blocking methods.

Soaking Method

This method is a great way to even out stitches and is especially good for sweaters that need plenty of shaping, such as the Bull's Eye. Fill the tub or sink with cold water. Submerge sweater in water and gently swirl to encourage stitches to relax. Remove from water, being careful not to stretch the item. Delicately squeeze out some of the water. Roll in a clean towel to remove excess water. Use rust-proof pins to pin pieces into the proper shape on a clean, dry towel. Take extra care with the edges, making sure they lay flat. Leave pinned to towel until dry.

Spraying Method

This method is faster and less involved than the soaking method but produces equally stunning results. Using rust-proof pins, pin pieces into proper shape on a clean, dry towel, taking extra care with edges. Lightly spray with water and let dry. You might want to use more water if knitting is stubborn. Leave pinned to towel until dry.

Steam Method

This is the quickest blocking method. Lay your pieces on a clean, dry towel, ironing board, or blocking board, with right sides facing down. Pin the pieces to their correct shape using rust-proof pins. Hold a steam iron over the pieces, being careful not to touch the iron to the fabric. You are not pressing the fabric! The heat and moisture will relax and straighten the stitches. Allow the pieces to cool to room temperature and to dry before picking them up.

KNITTING TECHNIQUES

MATTRESS STITCH

The mattress stitch is the perfect way to join vertical seams. Hold the two pieces to be joined next to each other, right sides facing up. Thread a tapestry needle with yarn. From the front, insert the needle under and out of the horizontal bar running between two stitches on one piece, then repeat the process on the corresponding stitch on the second piece. Keep working back and forth from side to side. Every few rows, stop and tug gently on the working yarn to draw the two sides together.

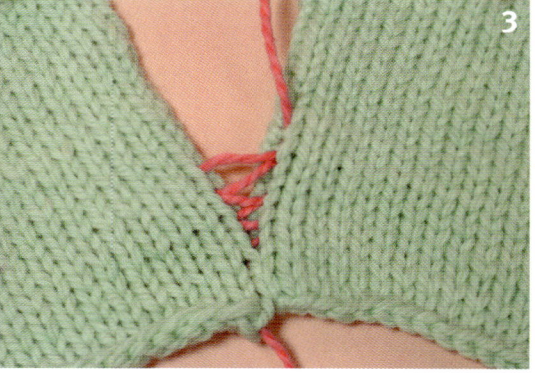

SINGLE CROCHET EDGING

To single crochet a border, place a slip knot on hook. Right side facing, starting at right corner (or left corner for lefties), *insert hook into next edge stitch and pull up a loop, then yarn over hook and pull through both loops on hook. Repeat from * across, placing stitches at intervals so that edge lies flat.

DUPLICATE STITCH

To duplicate stitch, thread a tapestry needle with a length of yarn. Insert the needle from back to front in the base of the stitch you want to cover, and pull it through. Working from the right side of the fabric, insert the needle around the base of the stitch above the one you want to cover, and pull the yarn through. Insert the needle back down into the fabric in the same place you started, and up again at the base of the next stitch. Continue this process for each of the stitches you want to embroider.

CROCHET CAST-ON

Make a slipknot on hook. Yarn over hook and bring a new loop through the chain you just made [one stitch on hook]. *Insert hook into slipknot and pull a new loop through. Grab yarn again and pull a loop through the first stitch on hook only.* You will begin to accumulate stitches on crochet hook. The slipknot will stretch to accommodate the new stitches and you'll be able to tighten it once you knit a few rows. Continue making stitches by repeating from * to * into slipknot until you have the desired number of stitches on your hook.

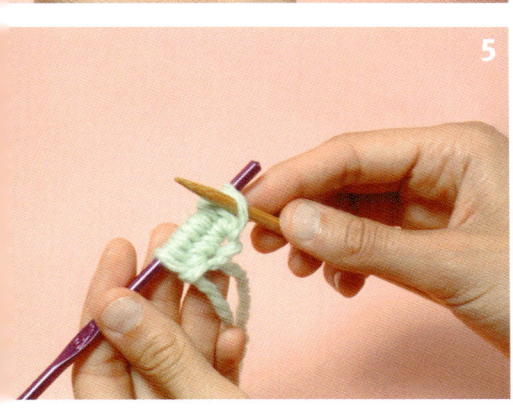

SINGLE CROCHET PIECES TOGETHER

To crochet pieces together, hold pieces wrong sides together. Place a slipknot on hook. Right side facing, starting at right corner (or left corner for lefties), *insert hook through both layers of fabric and pull up a loop, then yarn over hook and pull through both loops on hook. Repeat from * across.

SLIP SLIP KNIT

Slip next two stitches one at a time as to knit. Insert left needle into both stitches as to knit them, knit two together. SSK results in a left-leaning decrease.

PICKING UP STITCHES

To pick up stitches, *insert crochet hook into edge of knit fabric, wrap yarn around hook and pull through a loop. Place loop on knitting needle. Repeat from * until the desired number of stitches are on needle.

CASTING ON IN THE MIDDLE OF A ROW

Use the cable cast-on to cast on in the middle of a row. *Insert the right needle between the next two stitches on the left needle. Wrap the yarn around the needle and pull through a loop. Replace the loop on the left needle. Repeat from * until you have cast on the desired number of stitches.

INDEX

Abbreviations, 12
Argyle, definition, 64
Baabajoes Wool Pak Yarns NZ, 42
Blocking, 85
   soaking method, 85
   steam method, 85
   spraying method, 85
Blue Sky Alpacas yarn, 25, 26, 48
   cotton, 72
Casting on middle of row, 93
   crochet, 89
Complementary colors, 18
Dixie, profile, 63
Finnegan, profile, 69
Finishing/Care, 85
Gauge, 8
Harrisville Designs yarn, 53, 54
Jersey, definition, 24
Johnny, profile, 77
Kayla, profile, 50
Knitting techniques
   casting on, middle of row, 93
   crochet cast-on, 89
   duplicate stitch, 88
   mattress stitch, 86
   picking up stitches, 92
   single crochet edging, 87
   single crochet pieces together, 90
   slip slip knit, 91
Koigu Kersti yarn, 53, 54, 59, 60
Leash opening, 21
Lobster Pot Yarns, 15
Lorna's Laces yarn, 31, 32, 80
Mac, profile, 37
Manos del Uruguay yarn, 19, 20
Needles, knitting, 6

Oblique, definition, 14
Patterns,
   adjusting size to fit, 10
   Argyle Sweater, 65–68
   Baseball Jersey, 25–28
   Basic Sweater, 19–23
   Bull's Eye, 53–57
   Emboidered Dog Bed, 31–33
   Herringbone Jacket, 59–63
   Hoodie, 71–77
   Oblique Rib Scarf Set, 15–17
   Oblique Rib pattern, 17
   Patchwork Blanket, 79–85
   Polo Shirt, 41–45
   Ribbon Dress, 47–51
   Super-Warm Bulky Sweater, 35–38
Raglan sleeve, 25
   decrease, 27, 28
Sizing and measuring, 6
Skill levels key, 13
Stitches,
   duplicate, 88
   mattress stitch, 86
   patterns for any number of
      garter, 85
      garter stripe, 85
         garter ridges, 85
         herringbone, 61
         reverse stockinette, 85
         reverse stockinette stripe, 85
      stockinette, 8, 85
   patterns for 21,
      basket, 83
      dot, 83
      Eiffel tower, 84
      mock, 83

moss slip, 84
moss slip, two-color, 84
rice, 83
seed, 83
tweed, 82
woven, 82
woven, two-color, 82
patterns for 20,
1 x 1 rib, 82
2 x 2 check, 82
2 x 2 rib, 81
4 x 4 check, 82
eyelets, 82
oblique rib, 81
seed, 81

picking up stitches, 92
slip slip knit, 91
Symbols, 12
Swatches, calculating gauge from, 8
Washing knitted items, 11
Wyatt, profile, 29
Yarns
Baabajoes Wool Pak Yarns NZ, 42
Blue Sky Alpacas, 5, 26, 48
cotton, 72
Harrisville Designs, 53, 54
Koigu, 53, 54, 59, 60
Lobster Pot Yarns, 15, 16
Lorna's Laces, 31, 32, 80
Manos del Uruguay, 19, 20

Lucy *says, "It's a wrap!"*

ABOUT THE AUTHOR

Kimberly Hamlin has been knitting for many years. She lives in Brooklyn, New York, with her cat, Louis. The patterns in this book are Kim's creations. *Posh Pooches* is her first book.

ABOUT TRIXIE + PEANUT

trixie + peanut is a luxury pet boutique and on-line retailer located in New York City. trixie + peanut celebrates the unique relationship between pets and the people who love them. Named after founder Susan Bing's two rescued Boxers, trixie + peanut began as a mail-order catalog in 1999. trixie + peanut's flagship store was opened in November 2003, and it has since become a destination for discerning shoppers from all around the world.